HUGH BONNEVILLE

A COMPLETE BIOGRAPHY

OLIVER TAYLOR

TABLE OF CONTENTS

HUGH OR RICHARD?

He is now known as Lord Crawley, as he strolls around in white tie and tails, military or, on tartan, for weekends. Hugh Bonneville is best known for his portrayal of Lord Grantham on *Downton Abbey*, but before he became the cover image for blundering institutional ineptitude in *Twenty Twelve* and *W1A*, he played roles with deeper depth and range, such as a moving Philip Larkin and a ruthless partner in the BBC's *Daniel Deronda*.

The *Cazalets*, a dignified six-part tour of urbanites and ruralites alike as Britain readies itself to go it alone against Hitler, provided the necessary proof. The 2001 production of Elizabeth Jane Howard's book series finally made it to DVD after first airing all the way back in 2001. Bonneville, at the time, was still a promising actor who hoped to soon stop portraying unsuccessful suitors in dramas.

He has the right height, complexion, and manners to pass for the upper class. He can easily fit into any role even in a three-piece outfit. He has the potential to represent all the qualities that women want in their ideal television hero, including discretion and masculinity. There's only one catch.

Bonneville has ridden a wave of dolts and kooks to success. Do you remember that dreadful stockbroker from *Notting Hill* who didn't know who Julia Roberts was?
In other words, that's him there. His cheating wife was found under the sheets with Alessandro Nivola in the period drama *Mansfield Park*. Can we talk about *Thursday, the 12th*, the TV drama? It turns out that his wife was having an affair with Ciaran Hinds. Talk about the Tv drama, *Madame Bovary*, in which his spouse

betrays him by having an affair with Greg Wise.

Oddly, he takes on the characteristics of a different individual. Hugh Bonneville's true name is Hugh Williams.

However, after graduating from Cambridge and drama school, he decided to change it to Hugh Bonneville to reflect his newfound prominence as an actor and performer, while keeping his birth name for use in the world of writing and production.

Under one alias, he became a rising star at the RSC, while under the other he directed Jonathan Harvey's *Beautiful Thing* on London's West End and co-wrote a screenplay with actor-turned-director Christopher Luscombe. Before *American Beauty* came along, Sam Mendes was set to direct. Before *Charlotte Gray* came into the picture, Gillian Armstrong was almost in charge of directing.

The bearer of both identities was likely getting mixed up if Richard Bonneville was succeeding onstage and Hugh Williams was succeeding offstage.

And then, it happened at a party he went to, the host couldn't decide whether to address him as Hugh or Richard. The moment he realized the chaos, he made up his mind to stop it.
When he finally went by Hugh again, he was asked whether he was Richard's brother.

A SPY OR SECRET AGENT?

On November 10, 1963, Hugh Richard Bonneville Williams came into the world. His birthplace is Paddington, London. His parents career were medically affiliated. They were in no connection to his dream profession.

Bonneville's mom had a rather unique line of work. The 58-year-old actor's late mother, Patricia operated under *MI6* when he was a kid, a fact he was completely unaware of.

His mother was reluctant to discuss her career, even after she had retired, which prompted *Robert Crawley* to speculate that she "might have been a spy"

When he was about 10 years old, she broke the news to him that she had gotten a new job that would need her to be gone three days a week.

Little Hugh, got very sentimental and started crying. He threatened to leave the home, calling his mother "awful." It wasn't until many years later that he stumbled into the possibility that his mother had been working for British intelligence.

In the last three decades before her retirement, he had normalized dropping Patricia off at her Lambeth North office and waving her goodbye. When the word that the Century House MI6 building was going to be sold appeared in the press one day, he pointed to the picture and remarked, "...that's your office." His mother unhesitantly agreed. To satisfy his curiosity, he went on to ask whether she was a spy.

Patricia disputed. Hugh's mother, affectionately known as "the Colonel" by family, pals, and neighbours, passed away in 2015 at the age of 85, and he never learned the truth.

After her passing, the actor asked his father whether they had ever spoken about her job together, and he claimed she never brought it up.

He attended both the preparatory Dulwich College and the Dorset boarding school, Sherborne.

Bonneville attended Corpus Christi College, Cambridge, to study religion after finishing high school. He graduated with a lower grade in theology from Cambridge. After that, he attended London's Webber Douglas Academy of Dramatic Art to hone his acting skills.

Additionally, Bonneville attended and graduated from the National Youth Theatre.

IN THE SPHERE OF HOLLYWOOD

The Newbie on Set

The Open Air Theatre in Regent's Park is where Bonneville made his professional acting debut. The National Theatre welcomed him in 1987, and he featured in numerous plays there before he moved on to the famous and prestigious Royal Shakespeare Company in 1991.

There, he portrayed Laertes in Kenneth Branagh's *Hamlet* (1992–1993). In addition to his role as Surly in *The Alchemist*, his acting resume includes the roles of Valentine in *The Two Gentlemen of Verona* and Bergetto in *Tis Pity She's a Whore*.

Under the name Richard Bonneville, Bonneville had his debut appearance in the 1994 episode *The Dying Detective* of *The Memoirs of Sherlock Holmes*. Mary Shelley's *Frankenstein*, starring Robert De Niro and Kenneth Branagh, was his first feature picture.

Shelley's movie which featured Hugh as Schiller is about a medically-inclined student called Victor Frankenstein who brings a creature to life by assembling body parts from dead people. The science fiction horror film, at a budget of $45 million, earned $112 million worldwide.
Critics' remarks on the movie were divided.

After waiting for three years, he finally landed a job in the James Bond film *Tomorrow Never Dies*, playing a member of the air warfare force. Despite receiving poor reviews, the picture was able to do well at the box office, collecting over $333 million worldwide and placing it as the fourth highest-grossing film of 1997.

His early performances were often those of a lovably inept character, such as Bernie in the romantic drama, *Notting Hill* or Mr Rushworth in *Mansfield Park*, both of which were comedies (1999).

The Villain

Contrary to the decent roles he played in the '90s, he played the tyrannical Henleigh Grandcourt in *Daniel Deronda* (2002) and the psychotic murderer James Lampton in *The Commander* (2003). He also portrayed more evil roles in the BBC tv series *Take a Girl Like You* (2000) and *Armadillo* (2001). He portrayed Philip Larkin, a poet, in *Love Again*.

At the same time, he played a farmer in *High Heels and Low Lifes*, an action comedy-drama about two London women, Shannon (Minnie Driver) and Frances (Mary McCormack), who try to manipulate a team of gangsters spearheaded by Kerrigan (Michael Gambon) and Mason (Kevin McNally) into granting them £1,000,000 after they overhear a gang member's discussion during a local bank robbery.

Playing the young John Bayley opposite Kate Winslet in the biopic blockbuster film *Iris* (2001), which chronicled the marriage of novelist Iris Murdoch and her spouse John Bayley, he received critical acclaim and a nomination for a British Academy Film Award as the Best Supporting Actor for his performance. Reviews were mostly favourable, and the $16 million in revenue the picture made against its $5.5 million budget is a testament to that.

He portrayed Father Jack Dowling in the 2003 British drama film *Conspiracy of Lies*. The film, which examined chastity and its effects on the Catholic Church in the twenty-first century, won three international prizes.

Sir Christopher Wren was portrayed by Bonneville in the 2004 docudrama *Wren - The Man Who Built Britain*. In the same year, he also played Samuel Pepys in Stage Beauty, a love historical drama. Uncredited, he reprised his role as James Lampton in the 2005's production of *The Commander: Virus* and its sequel, *The Commander: Blackout*.

He also played Fraser McBride in the period drama film, *Man to Man*. The protagonist of the script is a member of a group of Victorian scientists doing fieldwork in Africa who starts to have second thoughts about the project's ethics.

In the 2006 British comedy-drama *Scenes of a Sexual Nature*, he played the role of Gerry. The film was inspired by seven unrelated love tales that took place on Hampstead Heath in north London. He was cast as Sebastian Burrows in 2007's *Four Last Songs* and as a painter in *Hola to the World*.

In addition to his roles in feature films, he has appeared in a few shorts. In 2004, he played Mr Burrell in *One of Those Days*, and in 2008, he played Jed in *French Film*.

The 2009 British thriller *Knife Edge* follows a wealthy Wall Street trader and her family as they move back to Britain, only to discover that their bucolic new house conceals a dark secret. Hugh played Charles Pollock in the thriller.

Hugh played Anne's actor buddy Gilbert Williams in the British military thriller film *Glorious Eye*. The plot tells the strong Keyes family as they try to maintain their conventional lifestyle on the brink of World War II, but their daughter Anne's life radically falls apart when she discovers secret recordings of the appeasement campaign.

In addition to his film and television career, Bonneville is also quite active in the radio industry.

In the BBC Radio 4 adaptation of John le Carré's book *The Honourable Schoolboy*, he portrayed Jerry Westerby. The adaptation originally aired in January 2010. He has previously been seen in the bizarre alternate-reality comedy *Married*.

Besides 'Downton Abbey'...

He played Robert, Earl of Grantham in the 2010–2015 ITV historical drama *Downton Abbey* and did the same in the 2019 film adaptation. He's been in a number of plays, but his performance in Downton was the one that made audiences feel the warmest toward him. The 6' 2" actor got all up thinking about the messages he received from fans who

16 | P a g e

stated *Downton Abbey* had supported them through tough times.

He's seen and read the letters of fans of his *Downton* show expressing gratitude to him for his performance which took them through happiness and as well created pleasant memories in their lives.

Hugh took out time to enjoy and have fun with his family (his wife of over 20 years, Lulu, and their teenage son, Felix), after the premiere of the film. Interestingly, the Royal family is also part of the large percentage of British families who are obsessed with TV series. The actors of the last season had a visit from Kate, the Duchess of Cambridge, and Sophie, the Countess of Wessex when they were filming at Ealing Studios.

Early in 2010, he had a cameo in the black comedy, *Burke and Hare*. The killings of Burke and Hare in 1828 served as inspiration for the British film. The $10 million budgeted comedy made $4.3 million at the movie office.

As Ben Sanger, he had a brief role in the American neo-noir *Shanghai*. The political thriller bombed at the movie office and was met with mostly unfavourable reviews upon its debut. This is the most poorly-rated film in which he has starred.

He played Ian Fletcher in the critically acclaimed BBC tv series *Twenty Twelve* from 2011 to 2012, and then again in the BBC television series *W1A* from 2014 to 2016. In the December 2012 episode of BBC Two's World's *Most Dangerous Roads*, he and co-star Jessica Hynes travelled across Georgia.

In addition, he co-starred alongside Cillian Murphy and Sienna Miller in the long-delayed picture *Hippie Hippie Shake*. Bonneville provided the voiceover for *The Hotel* on Channel 4 from 2011 through 2014.

In the films *Paddington* (2014) and *Paddington 2* (2017), Bonneville portrayed Mr Brown. In the Paddington books and movies, the title character is a humanoid bear named *Paddington* who moves from "Darkest Peru" to London and is fostered by the Brown family. The picture earned $282.8 million worldwide on a $54.7 million budget. In 2016, two years after the film's first release, Paddington was included at number 81 on *Empire magazine*'s list of the 100 finest British films.

During the 2015 and 2016 seasons, he played the humorous singing character of *The Pirate King* on the ABC classic comedy adventure series *Galavant*, which was inspired by fairy tales. He also provided the voiceover for the ITV show *The Cruise*. In *Muppets Most Wanted*, the Muppets' seventh theatrical picture, he portrayed an Irish journalist.

The criminal comedy made $80.4 million worldwide on a budget of $51 million, which was bad considering how popular its predecessor was. Notwithstanding, critics were likewise enthusiastic, praising the film's comedy, score, and emotional depth.

Bonneville also has audiobooks credited to him which contain his voice recordings of the Paddington tales.

In 2015, he lent his voice to the animated children's book *Stick Man*, playing the role of Santa Claus. The narrative depicts a humanoid wooden stick as he embarks on an Odyssey-like journey to go back to his family. In the end, his conversation with Santa Claus leads to his return to his "family tree" and the acceptance of his own family once more.

Viceroy's House (2017), directed by Gurinder Chadha, highlighted the turmoil and brutality accompanying the Partition of India during the last days of British control, and starred Bonneville as Lord Mountbatten.

With a budget of just $8.5 million, the period drama made $11.8 million. In the *Thomas &*

Friends: Journey Beyond Sodor, released in 2017, he provided the voice of Merlin.

Additionally, in that same year, it was revealed that Bonneville will portray Roald Dahl in a planned biopic about the author, of the documentary he voiced *A Return to Grace: Luther's Life and Legacy*. At the very least, five 2017 films include Bonneville, whose credits include the historical drama *Breathe*.
The film, starring Tom Hollander, portrays the true tale of Robin Cavendish, who at the age of 28 with polio and became crippled from the neck down.

In 2018, Bonneville took over for Julie Andrews as presenter and narrator of the Great Performances episode *"From Vienna: The New Year's Celebration"* which airs on PBS in the United States on New Year's Day. In the same year, he also reprised his role as Merlin for an episode of *Thomas & Friends'* twenty-second season.

Bonneville, Liz White, and Andrew Havill performed in the stage play *Shadowlands* at the Chichester Festival Theatre in 2019.

Hugh starred as the title character, Robert Crawley, in the 2019 period drama *Downton Abbey*. The drama penned by Fellowes illuminates a royal visit to the Crawley family's Yorkshire manor.

As members of the royal household have moved to Downton Abbey, a murderer also tags along with a concerted effort to take the monarch's life. The Queen's lady-in-waiting has parted out with the Crawley family, notably the Dowager Countess, over a property dispute, and she and the rest of the royal escort are set against the Crawleys and their servants.

The drama grossed the least difference of $100 million at the movie office earnings against its budgeted revenue.

Hugh played Dahl in the 2021 British drama film *To Olivia*, which was inspired by Stephen Michael Shearer's biography of Neal, titled *An Unquiet Life*. Opinions on the film were both favourable and unfavourable.

Reappearing as Robert Crawley in *Downton Abbey: A New Era* and portraying Mr Brown in the Paddington flicks are just two of Bonneville's recent appearances. In the next film *Paddington In Peru*, he will reprise his role for the third time.

I Came By

Hugh Bonneville is not the sort of guy who would murder a homosexual man, set fire to his corpse, and then flush the remains down the toilet. *I Came By* is the newest Netflix thriller, starring the actor of Paddington as a former high-ranking judge with an evil secret kept away in his attic.
He co-starred with George McKay and the *Line of Duty* star Kelly MacDonald.

It's like Psycho, the B-movie, but with a dash of social awareness, and it major theme that seems to be emerging in modern films: affluent people extremely crazy.
Even if this isn't the first time he's been cast in a part with a more sadistic rhythm, viewers who know him from *Downton Abbey* or *Paddington*, where he portrays the grouchy but ultimately beloved Mr Brown, will find this casting to be ironic.

Hugh, on the other hand, has been a part of at least 70 different TV shows, including many where he voiced characters.

On November 13 of this year, Hugh Bonneville will release his autobiography. The book, which will be titled *"Playing Under The Piano: From Downton To Darkest Peru,"* will chronicle Bonneville's whole profession, beginning with his performance in a school nativity and ending with his most well-known roles.

The memoir, which has been called "moving" and "laugh-out-loud," funny, will reflect on Bonneville's time spent working with such A-listers as Judi Dench, Julia Roberts, and Robert De Niro. It's also a sobering memoir of his life, including the challenges of coping with his father's illness and his mother's secret service job, which he learned about only after her demise.

Meanwhile, his work in *Iris, Tsunami: The Aftermath, Downton Abbey, Twenty Twelve, and W1A* has earned him no less than 20 nominations for various prizes. Nonetheless, the British actor took home three statuettes for his work in *Downton Abbey* and one for his part in *Iris*.

Hugh now plays the title role as The Mayor in the unreleased 3D computer-animated fantasy comedy film, The Amazing Maurice.

PERSONAL LIFE

While growing up in the same area of West Sussex, England, Bonneville and his future wife crossed paths. He and his family left the region a few years after they first met, and since then, they never saw one other again.

They reconnected after twenty-one years apart, and what happened next is the love story they share today.

Bonneville tied the knot with his entrepreneur-wife in her thirties when he met Lucinda "Lulu" Evans, who along with her sister in India manages the business *Indigo Island*. It took some time, but eventually, Hugh was able to create a family with the woman he loved. They have a son named Felix, and now the whole family resides in West Sussex. Felix, his son, has shown little interest in following in his father's footsteps in becoming an actor.

In the 2009 British premiere of *Kitty and Damnation* by Joseph Crilly for the Giant Olive Theatre Company at the Lion & Unicorn Theatre in Kentish Town, Bonneville lent his voice to the role of Justice Fosse.
A little time later, he became Giant Olive's very first patron. In addition to his work with *WaterAid*, Bonneville is a supporter of the London-based children's organisation *Scene & Heard*.

Bonneville was sworn in as a Deputy Lieutenant for West Sussex County on October 8, 2019. Thus, he was awarded the honorary lifetime title "DL". Hugh spends his leisure time volunteering with the South Downs National Park Trust, an organisation whose mission is to increase urban residents' appreciation for and use of the country.

Hugh's combat with Weight Loss

The *Downton Abbey* actor shocked his audience with his astonishing weight reduction improvement over the years as he adopted a healthier diet and started exercising regularly.

A year ago, when he made a virtual appearance on an episode of BBC's *The One* Show, people on Twitter commented on how physically fit the actor looked. Several folks then elaborated on why they couldn't recognise him. Hugh has always been transparent about the exercise routine he follows.

He discussed how he had lost almost a stone in weight before by altering his eating habits and engaging in more regular physical activity.

Hugh told the *Telegraph* previously that his trainer recommends he stay away from carbohydrates at night.

It is reported that low-carbohydrate diets are among the most successful approaches to losing weight.

Reduction of carb intake significantly may help one to lose weight without necessarily making any other changes to a diet or exercise routine.

Brown rice and brown bread are healthier options than white rice and white bread, but a reasonable quantity of carbohydrates could still be included in the regular diet.

The star stopped eating at three-hour intervals and instead ate smaller meals more often throughout the day. He also reduced his intake of items heavy in carbohydrates. This includes both savoury snacks like chips and candy and sweets like cookies and cake.

Substitution of lower-calorie options for high-carb items allows dieters to consume more food without gaining weight.

Hugh also often shares posts on social media about his efforts to be in shape. He often takes a walk out with his dog. Exercise is an essential component of any weight loss programme. because it causes one to burn calories at a faster rate,

As an added benefit, cardiovascular exercise like running has been shown to increase resting metabolic rate, which in turn increases calorie expenditure throughout the day.

DID YOU KNOW?

- Hugh is a towering 6 feet and 2 inches in stature.
- For the most part, Hugh prefers Chinese cuisine.
- Blue and hazel are his favourite hue.
- He has an estimated $8 million in wealth.
- Hugh favours conventional treatments since they run in his family; his father was a specialist, and his mother was a nurse. But he would hesitate to settle for an alternative medicine so long as it helps his back discomfort. As a kind of alternative rehabilitation, he embraces the concept of a sumo wrestler standing on his back frequently.
- The *downton* celebrity favours using the rail over a vehicle. He fantasizes about going through the Rockies on a train.
- On Rotten Tomatoes, his most highly rated performance in a film is his role

in *Paddington 2* in 2017 (for which he achieved a 99% approval rating), while his work in Shanghai in 2010 was met with the lowest approval rating of all of his film roles(4%).

- As a child, Hugh came to prefer summer above every other time of year. Presently, the 58-year-old looks forward to spring the most.

- Hugh has aspirations of being a minimalist but, in the meanwhile, is a chronic hoarder.

- Despite the fact that the English actor Hugh is in good shape, he is not successful at maintaining his healthy lifestyle. In addition to his daily yomp with the dogs, he also enjoys running and cycling. It's interesting that he has a habit of raiding the pantry at odd hours.

- Hugh enjoys travelling although he is becoming a homebody who enjoys putting the drawbridge on his gorgeous castle.

- He likened Kate Winslet, who starred with him in the 2001 film *Iris*, as "a force of nature."
- Minnie Driver, Julian Fellowes, Rupert Friend, Matthew Goode, Angela Lansbury, Sue Johnston, and Terence Stamp are all graduates of London's Webber Douglas Academy of Dramatic Art.
- Fortunately, he can communicate in French.
- Some of his favourite comedies on television include *Rev.* (2010) and *Curb Your Enthusiasm* (2000).
- He has appeared in films from both the *Doctor Who* and *Eon* James Bond series.
- *Cloaca*, at the Old Vic Theatre in London, featured him prominently in the fall of 2004.
- He is often confused with Paul Burrell, the former butler of Princess Diana, and Colin Firth, another British actor.

- Because he believes that people's viewpoints are not enthusiastically appreciated, Hugh finds it "painful" to be actively participating in Twitter.
- The native Londoner has a soft spot for rural life.

SUMMARY

Hugh Richard Bonneville Williams's parents, a urological specialist and a nurse welcomed him into the world on November 10, 1963, in Paddington, London, England.

After finishing preparatory school, he enrolled in the independent Sherborne School.He attended Corpus Christi College, Cambridge, after completing his secondary schooling. After that, Bonneville attended the Webber Douglas Academy of Dramatic Art to hone his acting skills.

At the beginning of his career as an actor, Hugh Bonneville made his debut at the Open Air Theatre. He joined the National Theatre company in 1987 and has since performed in a number of productions there.

Chancer, a 1990 drama series, was his first appearance on television. About a year later, the actor was cast in a performance of *Hamlet* by the Royal Shakespeare Company.He got his first acting gig in the 1994 adaptation of Mary Shelley's *Frankenstein.*

A mere two years later, Bonneville appeared in the ill-fated comedy *Married for Life*. He went on to star in *Get Well Soon* and *Mosely* on TV in the years that followed. At the end of the decade, he had a cameo in the romantic drama *Mansfield Park.*

Beginning the new millennium with an appearance in *Take a Girl Like You* a comedy series, Bonneville proved himself in the new millennium. The three-part miniseries aired on *HBO* and was based on Kingsley Amis's 1960 book of the same name.

Over the following years, he guest starred on a wide variety of shows including *The*

Cazalets, Courting Alex, and *The Robinsons.* In the same year, the actor's work in the TV movie *Tsunami: The Aftermath* won him a Golden Nymph Award.

He was the voice of the documentary series *Country House Rescue* from its inception in 2008 until its last episode in 2011. At the period, Bonneville also appeared in the films *French Film, Knife Edge,* and *From Time to Time.*

In 2011, he also became a part of the cast of the BBC comedy series *Twenty Twelve* and started voicing the documentary *The Hotel.*

In *Paddington* a live-action animated comedy film based on Michael Bond's character Paddington Bear, he played Mr Henry Brown. In 2017, a sequel to Paddington was published, and he returned to the role.

Beginning in 2015, Bonneville has provided his voice to the cartoon series *Sofia the First.*

For ITV's reality show *The Cruise* he has been the voiceover since 2016.

In the 2001 British-American biopic *Iris*, Hugh Bonneville portrays the young literary critic John Bayley in the biography of English author Dame Iris Murdoch and her connection with Bayley. His portrayal in the film garnered Bonneville nods for both the British Academy of Film and Television Arts and the European Film Award.

In the ITV period drama, *Downton Abbey* the actor portrayed Robert Crawley, Earl of Grantham, from 2010 until 2015. As a result of his performance, he was nominated for many prestigious awards.

In 1998, Hugh Bonneville wed Lucinda Evans. Today they are proud parents to Felix, their son.

Currently, Hugh is working towards publishing his memoir and starring in more blockbuster films and dramas that will blow up the box office like the Downton Abbey series.

Printed in Great Britain
by Amazon

37217369R00030